Lessons in Entrepreneurship: Learning from Business Mistakes

Raymond Jack

Copyright © [2023]

Title: Lessons in Entrepreneurship: Learning from Business Mistakes
Author's: Raymond Jack

All rights reserved. No part of this publication may be reproduced, stored in a retrieval system, or transmitted in any form or by any means, electronic, mechanical, photocopying, recording, or otherwise, without the prior written permission of the publisher or author, except in the case of brief quotations embodied in critical reviews and certain other non-commercial uses permitted by copyright law.

This book was printed and published by [Publisher's: **Raymond Jack**] in [2023]

ISBN:

TABLE OF CONTENT

Chapter 1: Introduction to Entrepreneurship — 06

Understanding the Entrepreneurial Mindset

Importance of Learning from Business Mistakes

Chapter 2: The Power of Failure — 11

Embracing Failure as a Learning Opportunity

Overcoming the Fear of Failure

Chapter 3: Common Business Mistakes to Avoid — 15

Lack of Market Research and Analysis

Poor Financial Management

Ineffective Marketing Strategies

Ignoring Customer Feedback

Chapter 4: Case Studies in Business Mistakes   23

The Rise and Fall of Blockbuster

Lessons from the Dot-Com Bubble

Kodak: A Story of Missed Opportunities

Chapter 5: Learning from Personal Mistakes   29

Overcoming Challenges in Starting a Business

The Importance of Adaptability and Flexibility

Building a Strong Support Network

Chapter 6: Strategies for Success   35

Developing a Growth Mindset

Continuous Learning and Professional Development

Finding Mentors and Role Models

Chapter 7: The Road to Entrepreneurial Success   41

Setting Realistic Goals and Milestones

Perseverance and Resilience in the Face of Setbacks

Celebrating Achievements and Learning from Successes

Chapter 8: Conclusion   47

Final Thoughts on Learning from Business Mistakes

Taking Action and Applying Lessons Learned

Chapter 1: Introduction to Entrepreneurship

Understanding the Entrepreneurial Mindset

In the fiercely competitive world of business, having the right mindset is crucial for success. The entrepreneurial mindset is a unique way of thinking that sets entrepreneurs apart from the rest. It involves a combination of traits, attitudes, and behaviors that enable individuals to identify opportunities, take calculated risks, and turn their ideas into thriving ventures.

This subchapter aims to provide students with a comprehensive understanding of the entrepreneurial mindset and how it can be cultivated. By learning from the mistakes of established entrepreneurs, students can gain valuable insights into the mindset required to navigate the challenges and uncertainties of the business world.

1. Embracing Failure: One of the key aspects of the entrepreneurial mindset is the ability to embrace failure as a learning opportunity. Successful entrepreneurs understand that failure is not a setback but rather a stepping stone towards success. By examining the mistakes and missteps of others, students can develop resilience and learn to view failures as valuable experiences that contribute to personal and professional growth.

2. Persistence and Determination: Entrepreneurs often face numerous obstacles and setbacks along their journey. The entrepreneurial mindset requires unwavering persistence and determination to overcome these challenges. By studying the stories of entrepreneurs who have encountered failure but persevered,

students can develop the mindset necessary to push through difficult times and remain focused on their goals.

3. Taking Calculated Risks: Entrepreneurs are known for their ability to take calculated risks. However, it is crucial to differentiate between reckless risk-taking and strategic decision-making. By examining the mistakes made by entrepreneurs who took unnecessary risks, students can gain insights into the importance of conducting thorough research, analyzing market trends, and making informed decisions.

4. Adaptability and Flexibility: The business landscape is constantly evolving, and successful entrepreneurs understand the importance of adaptability and flexibility. Studying the mistakes made by entrepreneurs who failed to adapt to changing market conditions can help students develop the mindset required to identify emerging trends, pivot their strategies, and seize new opportunities.

5. Vision and Innovation: Entrepreneurs are driven by a vision and a desire to create something new and innovative. By learning from the mistakes of entrepreneurs who failed to innovate or lacked a clear vision, students can develop an entrepreneurial mindset that values creativity, forward-thinking, and the ability to identify gaps in the market.

In conclusion, understanding the entrepreneurial mindset is vital for students who aspire to venture into the world of business. By learning from the mistakes of established entrepreneurs, students can gain valuable insights into the mindset required to succeed. Embracing failure, persistence, taking calculated risks, adaptability, and vision are key pillars of the entrepreneurial mindset that can be cultivated through learning from the mistakes of others.

Importance of Learning from Business Mistakes

In the fast-paced world of entrepreneurship, success is often accompanied by a series of failures and mistakes. As students venturing into the realm of business, it is crucial to understand the importance of learning from these mistakes. In the subchapter titled "Importance of Learning from Business Mistakes" in the book "Lessons in Entrepreneurship: Learning from Business Mistakes," we delve into the significance of embracing failures and turning them into valuable learning experiences.

Mistakes are inevitable in any business venture. They may range from minor setbacks to major failures that can shake the very foundation of your entrepreneurial dreams. However, it is essential to realize that mistakes are not the end but rather stepping stones towards growth and success. Each failure provides an opportunity to reflect, analyze, and improve upon the shortcomings that led to the mistake.

One of the primary reasons why learning from mistakes is crucial is the knowledge gained through firsthand experience. Classroom education may provide a theoretical understanding of various business concepts, but it is in the real world that these principles truly come to life. Mistakes offer a hands-on education that cannot be replicated in any textbook or lecture hall. By analyzing our failures, we gain valuable insights into the intricacies of running a business, enabling us to make better decisions in the future.

Learning from mistakes also fosters resilience and adaptability, two qualities essential for success in the ever-evolving business landscape. When faced with failure, it is essential to embrace it as an opportunity for growth rather than succumbing to despair. By developing a mindset that perceives mistakes as valuable learning experiences, students can cultivate the resilience needed to bounce back from setbacks and adapt their strategies to overcome challenges.

Moreover, learning from mistakes helps to avoid repetition of the same errors. By carefully analyzing the causes of failure, students can identify patterns and make necessary adjustments to their approach. This iterative process of trial and error is a fundamental aspect of entrepreneurship, allowing for continuous improvement and innovation.

In conclusion, the subchapter on the "Importance of Learning from Business Mistakes" in the book "Lessons in Entrepreneurship: Learning from Business Mistakes" emphasizes the significance of embracing failures as learning opportunities. By understanding the knowledge gained through mistakes, fostering resilience, and avoiding repetition, students can develop a solid foundation for their entrepreneurial journey. Remember, the road to success is paved with failures, and it is through learning from these mistakes that true growth and achievement are realized.

Chapter 2: The Power of Failure

Embracing Failure as a Learning Opportunity

Failure is often seen as something to be avoided at all costs. It is associated with shame, disappointment, and a fear of taking risks. However, in the world of entrepreneurship, failure is not only inevitable but also a valuable learning opportunity. In this subchapter, we will explore the concept of embracing failure and how it can be a powerful tool for personal and professional growth.

As students, we are often conditioned to strive for perfection and success. We are taught to fear failure and to avoid making mistakes. However, the reality is that mistakes are an integral part of the learning process. When we embrace failure, we open ourselves up to new possibilities and opportunities for growth.

One of the greatest benefits of embracing failure is the chance to learn from our mistakes. Each failure provides us with valuable insights and lessons that can be applied to future endeavors. By analyzing what went wrong and why, we can gain a deeper understanding of ourselves, our strengths, and our weaknesses. This self-awareness is crucial for personal and professional development.

Embracing failure also helps to build resilience and perseverance. It teaches us how to bounce back from setbacks and keep moving forward. Successful entrepreneurs understand that failure is not the end but a stepping stone towards success. They view failure as a necessary part of the journey, not a reflection of their worth or abilities.

Furthermore, embracing failure encourages innovation and creativity. When we are not afraid to take risks and make mistakes, we are more likely to think outside the box and come up with groundbreaking ideas. Failure pushes us out of our comfort zones and forces us to explore new approaches and solutions.

To truly embrace failure as a learning opportunity, it is important to adopt a growth mindset. A growth mindset recognizes that intelligence and abilities can be developed through dedication and hard work. Instead of seeing failure as a reflection of our abilities, we see it as a chance to learn and improve.

In conclusion, embracing failure as a learning opportunity is vital for anyone aspiring to be an entrepreneur. By reframing failure as a stepping stone towards success, we can harness its power to learn, grow, and innovate. As students, it is important to understand that failure is not something to be feared but embraced. It is through our mistakes that we can truly excel and make a difference in the world of business.

Overcoming the Fear of Failure

Introduction:

One of the most significant obstacles on the path to success is the fear of failure. This fear can paralyze even the most determined individuals, preventing them from taking risks and pursuing their dreams. However, in the world of entrepreneurship, failure is often seen as a stepping stone towards success. In this subchapter, we will explore how to overcome the fear of failure and embrace it as a valuable learning experience.

1. Understanding the Nature of Failure:

It is crucial for students and aspiring entrepreneurs to understand that failure is not the end but rather a part of the journey. Many successful entrepreneurs have experienced multiple failures before achieving their goals. Failure allows us to learn from our mistakes, gain experience, and refine our strategies. It is a necessary and inevitable aspect of any entrepreneurial endeavor.

2. Changing Your Perspective:

Instead of viewing failure as a negative outcome, it is important to reframe our perspective. Failure should be seen as a learning opportunity, a chance to grow and improve. Embracing failure means embracing the process of trial and error, where each mistake brings us closer to success. By shifting our mindset, we can transform failure into a stepping stone towards achieving our entrepreneurial dreams.

3. Analyzing and Learning from Mistakes:

When failure occurs, it is crucial to analyze the situation and identify the factors that led to the outcome. By reflecting on our mistakes, we can learn valuable lessons that will guide us in future endeavors. Successful entrepreneurs often use failure as a means to improve their decision-making process, refine their strategies, and adapt to changing circumstances. By embracing failure, students can develop resilience and become more equipped to handle future challenges.

4. Seeking Support:

Overcoming the fear of failure can be an overwhelming task, especially for students who are still learning and exploring their entrepreneurial potential. Surrounding yourself with a support network of like-minded individuals, mentors, or entrepreneurs who have experienced failure can be immensely helpful. Sharing experiences, seeking advice, and learning from others' mistakes can provide valuable insights and guidance on overcoming the fear of failure.

Conclusion:

Overcoming the fear of failure is an essential step towards becoming a successful entrepreneur. By understanding the nature of failure, changing our perspective, analyzing mistakes, and seeking support, students can learn from their mistakes and use failure as a catalyst for growth. Embracing failure as a valuable learning experience will empower aspiring entrepreneurs to take risks, pursue their dreams, and ultimately achieve success. Remember, failure is not the end but a stepping stone on the path to greatness.

Chapter 3: Common Business Mistakes to Avoid

Lack of Market Research and Analysis

Market research and analysis are crucial components of any successful business venture. However, many entrepreneurs often overlook or underestimate their importance, leading to significant mistakes and potential failure. In this subchapter, we will explore the consequences of a lack of market research and analysis, and how students can learn from these mistakes to build thriving businesses.

One of the most common mistakes made by budding entrepreneurs is assuming that their idea or product will automatically find a market. They tend to rely on personal opinions or anecdotal evidence, without conducting proper research to validate their assumptions. This lack of market research can result in a mismatch between the product or service offered and the target audience's actual needs and preferences.

Without understanding the market landscape, entrepreneurs may struggle to position their offerings effectively, leading to poor sales and wasted resources. Moreover, they may fail to identify potential competitors and differentiate their products or services from existing ones. This lack of analysis can hinder growth and prevent the establishment of a unique selling proposition.

Learning from these mistakes is crucial for students aspiring to become successful entrepreneurs. By recognizing the significance of market research and analysis, they can avoid falling into the same trap. Students should be encouraged to conduct thorough market research to identify their target audience, understand their needs and preferences, and assess the viability of their business ideas.

Furthermore, it is essential to teach students how to analyze market data and trends to make informed decisions. By studying the competition and industry dynamics, students can identify gaps in the market, develop innovative solutions, and position their offerings effectively.

In conclusion, the lack of market research and analysis is a significant mistake that entrepreneurs often make, resulting in failed business ventures. By addressing this issue, students can learn valuable lessons and avoid making the same mistakes. Through proper market research, analysis, and understanding of their target audience, students can lay the foundation for successful entrepreneurship. By emphasizing the importance of market research and analysis early on, students can develop the skills necessary to build thriving businesses in the future.

Poor Financial Management

One of the critical aspects of running a successful business is managing finances effectively. However, poor financial management is a common mistake that many entrepreneurs make, often leading to disastrous consequences. In this subchapter, we will explore the pitfalls of poor financial management and the valuable lessons we can learn from these mistakes.

Financial management encompasses various activities, including budgeting, cash flow management, financial planning, and accounting. Failing to pay attention to these aspects can have severe repercussions on your business's long-term sustainability. Let's delve into some of the key mistakes entrepreneurs make in this area and the lessons we can derive from them.

Firstly, neglecting to create a solid budget can spell disaster for any business. Without a clear understanding of your income and expenses, you may find yourself overspending or misallocating funds, leading to financial instability. The lesson here is simple: always create a comprehensive budget that accurately reflects your anticipated income and expenses, and regularly review and adjust it as necessary.

Secondly, poor cash flow management can cripple even the most promising ventures. Entrepreneurs often make the mistake of not monitoring their cash flow effectively, resulting in a lack of funds to cover essential expenses or seize growth opportunities. The key lesson is to develop robust cash flow forecasting techniques, closely monitor your inflows and outflows, and establish contingency plans to address any shortfalls.

Another common financial management mistake is the failure to plan for the future. Entrepreneurs may become too focused on the present, neglecting to save or invest for growth or unforeseen circumstances. It is crucial to regularly set aside funds for emergencies, expansion, and reinvestment. Always remember that failing to plan for the future is planning to fail.

Lastly, inadequate accounting practices can lead to significant financial setbacks. Neglecting to maintain accurate and up-to-date financial records can result in cash discrepancies, errors in tax filings, and missed opportunities for deductions or cost savings. The lesson here is to prioritize proper accounting practices, whether by hiring a professional accountant or using reliable accounting software, to ensure accurate financial reporting and decision-making.

In conclusion, poor financial management is a mistake that can have dire consequences for any business. By learning from these mistakes and implementing effective financial management practices, you can avoid financial pitfalls and set your business on the path to success. Remember to create a comprehensive budget, manage cash flow diligently, plan for the future, and prioritize accurate accounting. By doing so, you will be well-equipped to navigate the financial challenges that entrepreneurs often face and build a solid foundation for your entrepreneurial journey.

Ineffective Marketing Strategies

In the competitive world of business, marketing plays a crucial role in the success of any venture. It is the key to reaching out to potential customers, creating brand awareness, and ultimately driving sales. However, not all marketing strategies prove to be effective. In this subchapter, we will delve into some common ineffective marketing strategies that entrepreneurs should avoid, and the valuable lessons that can be learned from these mistakes.

One of the most prevalent mistakes entrepreneurs make is a lack of target audience identification. A misguided attempt to appeal to a broad audience often results in a diluted message that fails to resonate with anyone. It is essential to conduct thorough market research and identify the specific needs and preferences of the target audience. By understanding their demographics, interests, and pain points, entrepreneurs can tailor their marketing efforts to address these specific needs effectively.

Another ineffective marketing strategy is poor communication and inconsistent messaging. Many entrepreneurs fail to convey a clear and compelling message that differentiates their product or service from the competition. Without a unique selling proposition, potential customers fail to see the value in what is being offered. Consistency in messaging across all marketing channels is paramount to build brand recognition and trust.

In today's digital age, online marketing has become essential. However, a common mistake is relying solely on one platform or channel. Entrepreneurs must diversify their marketing efforts and utilize multiple platforms to reach a wider audience. Relying solely on social media, for example, may limit reach and exposure to potential customers. A multi-channel approach that incorporates social media, email marketing, content marketing, and search engine optimization can yield better results.

Furthermore, failing to track and measure marketing efforts is a grave mistake. Without proper analytics and metrics in place, entrepreneurs cannot determine which strategies are effective and which ones are not. It is crucial to track website traffic, conversion rates, and customer engagement to gain insights into the effectiveness of marketing campaigns. This data enables entrepreneurs to make informed decisions and optimize their strategies accordingly.

In conclusion, effective marketing is essential for business success. However, certain strategies can prove to be ineffective if not executed properly. By avoiding the mistakes mentioned above and learning from these experiences, entrepreneurs can develop more effective marketing strategies and achieve their business goals. Remember, effective marketing is about understanding the target audience, delivering a clear message, diversifying marketing efforts, and tracking performance.

Ignoring Customer Feedback

In the realm of entrepreneurship, ignoring customer feedback is a grave mistake that can have serious consequences for the success of a business. Customer feedback is a valuable source of information that provides insights into the needs, preferences, and satisfaction levels of consumers. It allows entrepreneurs to gauge the effectiveness of their products or services, identify areas for improvement, and ultimately build customer loyalty. However, despite its importance, many entrepreneurs fail to recognize the significance of customer feedback, leading to detrimental outcomes.

One of the main reasons entrepreneurs ignore customer feedback is due to a lack of understanding of its value. Students embarking on their entrepreneurial journey must recognize that customer feedback is an invaluable tool for growth and development. By actively seeking and listening to customer feedback, entrepreneurs gain insights into the strengths and weaknesses of their offerings, enabling them to make informed decisions. Ignoring this feedback can result in missed opportunities for improvement and innovation, ultimately hindering the growth of the business.

Another reason entrepreneurs disregard customer feedback is the fear of criticism. Negative feedback can be difficult to accept, as it may challenge an entrepreneur's vision and efforts. However, it is important to remember that constructive criticism is an opportunity for growth. By acknowledging and addressing customer concerns, entrepreneurs can enhance their products or services, thereby increasing customer satisfaction and loyalty. Students should embrace feedback as a chance to learn and adapt, recognizing that it is an integral part of the entrepreneurial journey.

Furthermore, ignoring customer feedback can lead to a disconnect between the entrepreneur and their target market. Students must understand that their customers are the lifeblood of their business, and their needs should be at the forefront of decision-making. By actively engaging with customers and valuing their feedback, entrepreneurs can foster a strong and loyal customer base, which is essential for long-term success.

In conclusion, ignoring customer feedback is a critical mistake that entrepreneurs should avoid at all costs. By recognizing the value of customer feedback, understanding that constructive criticism is an opportunity for growth, and prioritizing customer needs, students can learn from this mistake and build successful businesses. Embracing customer feedback as a learning tool will enable entrepreneurs to continuously improve their offerings, enhance customer satisfaction, and thrive in the competitive landscape of entrepreneurship.

Chapter 4: Case Studies in Business Mistakes

The Rise and Fall of Blockbuster

Blockbuster, once a giant in the entertainment industry, serves as a cautionary tale for entrepreneurs and business leaders alike. This subchapter delves into the rise and fall of Blockbuster, highlighting the valuable lessons we can learn from its mistakes.

In the late 1980s, Blockbuster emerged as a dominant force in the video rental market. With its vast selection of movies and convenient store locations, it seemed unstoppable. However, as technology advanced and the internet became more prevalent, Blockbuster failed to adapt and embrace change.

One crucial mistake Blockbuster made was underestimating the potential of online streaming. In 2000, Reed Hastings, the founder of Netflix, proposed a partnership to Blockbuster, suggesting they could collaborate and revolutionize the video rental industry. Blockbuster, blinded by its success and confident in its traditional business model, rejected the offer. This decision would ultimately prove fatal.

As the popularity of DVDs and streaming services grew, Blockbuster's reliance on physical stores became its downfall. The company failed to recognize the shift in consumer behavior towards online rentals and the convenience of home entertainment. By the time Blockbuster attempted to catch up by introducing its own online platform, it was too late. Netflix had already established itself as the industry leader.

Another critical mistake Blockbuster made was disregarding customer preferences. While Netflix introduced a subscription-based model with no late fees, Blockbuster continued to charge exorbitant late fees, frustrating its customers and driving them away. This failure to listen to its customers' demands and adapt to market changes ultimately led to its demise.

The lessons we can learn from the rise and fall of Blockbuster are invaluable. First and foremost, entrepreneurs must never become complacent, even when experiencing success. The business landscape is constantly evolving, and failing to adapt can have dire consequences.

Furthermore, entrepreneurs must embrace innovation and be open to partnerships and collaborations. Blockbuster's refusal to work with Netflix prevented them from capitalizing on emerging trends and seizing new opportunities.

Finally, listening to customers is vital. Understanding their preferences, needs, and desires is crucial for long-term success. By neglecting customer feedback and failing to meet their changing demands, Blockbuster lost its customer base and ultimately its relevance.

In conclusion, the rise and fall of Blockbuster is a powerful case study in the importance of adaptability, innovation, and customer-centricity. Entrepreneurs and students alike can learn from Blockbuster's mistakes, ensuring they are better equipped to navigate the ever-changing business landscape and avoid a similar fate.

Lessons from the Dot-Com Bubble

The Dot-Com Bubble, also known as the Internet Bubble, was a significant period in the late 1990s and early 2000s where the stock market experienced a massive surge in investment and speculation in internet-based companies. This fervor led to a valuation bubble that eventually burst, resulting in the collapse of many dot-com companies and enormous financial losses for investors.

For students interested in entrepreneurship and learning from mistakes, the Dot-Com Bubble offers invaluable lessons. It serves as a cautionary tale, highlighting the importance of understanding market dynamics, long-term sustainability, and the perils of irrational exuberance. Here are some key takeaways from this historic event:

1. Market Awareness: The Dot-Com Bubble created an environment where investors poured money into companies with little to no revenue or proven business models. It teaches students the significance of thoroughly understanding the market, identifying profitable opportunities, and conducting due diligence before investing time and resources into a venture.

2. Sustainable Growth: Many companies during the dot-com era focused on achieving rapid growth without considering profitability. This approach ultimately proved unsustainable. Students should learn the importance of balancing growth with profitability, as sustainable businesses require a solid revenue stream to survive and thrive in the long run.

3. Realistic Valuations: The Dot-Com Bubble witnessed sky-high valuations for companies with limited or no profits. It is crucial for

students to understand the significance of realistic valuation methods based on fundamentals, such as revenue, profit margins, and market potential. Overvaluing a company can lead to financial instability and unrealistic expectations.

4. Timing and Patience: The Dot-Com Bubble also teaches students about the importance of timing and patience. Many companies failed to weather the storm because they ran out of financial resources before the market had a chance to mature. Students should learn to exercise patience, not rush into ventures without a solid foundation, and be prepared for market fluctuations.

5. Adaptability and Innovation: While the Dot-Com Bubble resulted in significant losses, it also marked a period of immense technological innovation. Students should recognize the importance of adaptability and staying ahead of the curve, as successful entrepreneurs are those who can evolve their business models to meet changing market demands.

In conclusion, the lessons from the Dot-Com Bubble provide valuable insights for students interested in entrepreneurship and learning from mistakes. By understanding the pitfalls of the past, students can develop a more informed and strategic approach to navigating the ever-changing business landscape.

Kodak: A Story of Missed Opportunities

In the world of entrepreneurship, success is often accompanied by a series of failures and mistakes. Learning from these missteps is crucial for aspiring business owners and entrepreneurs. This subchapter titled "Kodak: A Story of Missed Opportunities" explores the journey of a once-giant in the photography industry, Kodak, and the valuable lessons we can learn from its downfall.

Kodak, founded in the late 19th century, revolutionized the photography industry with its innovative products and services. For decades, it dominated the market, becoming a household name synonymous with photography. However, despite its early success, Kodak failed to adapt to the rapidly evolving digital landscape, ultimately leading to its demise.

One of the primary mistakes Kodak made was its failure to recognize and embrace the digital revolution. In the 1970s, Kodak engineer Steve Sasson developed the world's first digital camera. However, the company's top executives were hesitant to invest in this groundbreaking technology, fearing it would cannibalize their lucrative film business. This decision proved to be a fatal mistake, as digital photography soon became the new norm, rendering film obsolete.

Another missed opportunity for Kodak was its inability to leverage its extensive patent portfolio effectively. The company held numerous patents related to digital imaging, but instead of capitalizing on them, it chose to focus on traditional film-based products. Kodak's failure to monetize its intellectual property and adapt to emerging market trends allowed competitors such as Canon and Sony to gain a significant advantage in the digital photography market.

Furthermore, Kodak's reluctance to enter the online photo-sharing space was yet another missed opportunity. In the early 2000s, platforms like Flickr and later Instagram gained immense popularity, revolutionizing how people shared and consumed photographs. Kodak, however, failed to recognize the potential of these platforms and neglected to develop its own online photo-sharing service. By the time the company attempted to enter this space, it was already too late, and competitors had established a strong presence.

The story of Kodak serves as a cautionary tale for entrepreneurs. It highlights the importance of staying ahead of market trends, adapting to technological advancements, and being willing to take calculated risks. The failure to innovate and embrace change can lead to missed opportunities and ultimately, the downfall of even the most established businesses.

As students of entrepreneurship, it is essential to learn from Kodak's mistakes. By studying this case, we can cultivate a mindset that values innovation, flexibility, and strategic decision-making. Understanding the lessons from Kodak's missed opportunities allows us to navigate the ever-changing business landscape with a more comprehensive perspective, increasing our chances of success as entrepreneurs.

Chapter 5: Learning from Personal Mistakes

Overcoming Challenges in Starting a Business

Starting a business is an exciting endeavor that requires passion, dedication, and a strong vision. However, it is not without its fair share of challenges. In this subchapter, we will explore some of the common obstacles that entrepreneurs face when starting their own venture and discuss effective strategies to overcome them. By learning from the mistakes of others, students can gain valuable insights and increase their chances of success in their entrepreneurial journey.

One of the primary challenges in starting a business is the lack of experience. Many students may have theoretical knowledge but lack practical know-how. This can lead to poor decision-making, ineffective management, and financial difficulties. To overcome this challenge, it is crucial to seek mentorship and guidance from experienced entrepreneurs. Engaging in internships, attending workshops, and connecting with industry professionals can provide invaluable insights into the real-world challenges of running a business.

Another challenge is the fear of failure. Starting a business involves taking risks, and the fear of failure can be paralyzing. However, it is important to remember that failure is a natural part of the entrepreneurial journey. By reframing failure as a learning opportunity, students can develop resilience and adaptability. Embracing a growth mindset and viewing mistakes as valuable lessons will help them bounce back stronger and make better-informed decisions.

Financial constraints are also a significant hurdle for aspiring entrepreneurs. Lack of capital can limit the scope and potential of a business. However, instead of viewing it as an obstacle, students can consider alternative funding sources such as crowdfunding, grants, or partnerships. Bootstrapping, or starting with minimal resources, can also be a viable option. By being resourceful and creative, students can find innovative ways to finance their business ideas.

Lastly, building a strong network and finding the right team can be challenging for students. Surrounding oneself with like-minded individuals who share the same passion and drive is crucial for success. Networking events, industry conferences, and online communities can provide opportunities to connect with potential partners, investors, and mentors.

In conclusion, starting a business is not without its challenges, but by learning from the mistakes of others, students can be better prepared to overcome them. The lack of experience, fear of failure, financial constraints, and building a network are some of the common hurdles faced by entrepreneurs. By seeking guidance, embracing failure as a learning opportunity, exploring alternative funding sources, and networking strategically, students can navigate these challenges more effectively. Remember, entrepreneurship is a journey, and perseverance, adaptability, and continuous learning are key to overcoming obstacles and achieving success.

The Importance of Adaptability and Flexibility

Subchapter: The Importance of Adaptability and Flexibility

Introduction:
In the fast-paced world of entrepreneurship, success often hinges on one's ability to adapt and be flexible. As aspiring entrepreneurs, it is crucial for students like you to understand the importance of these traits. In this subchapter, we will delve into the significance of adaptability and flexibility and explore how learning from business mistakes can help you develop these essential skills.

Why Adaptability Matters:
In today's dynamic business landscape, change is the only constant. Businesses that fail to adapt risk becoming irrelevant or obsolete. Adaptability allows entrepreneurs to respond effectively to unforeseen challenges and capitalize on emerging opportunities. By being adaptable, you can navigate through uncertainties, pivot your strategies, and stay ahead of the curve. Learning from business mistakes enables you to analyze past failures, identify areas that require adaptation, and develop a growth mindset, enabling you to thrive in an ever-changing environment.

The Power of Flexibility:
Flexibility is closely intertwined with adaptability. It involves being open-minded, embracing new ideas, and adjusting your approach as circumstances demand. An inflexible mindset can hinder progress and limit creativity. On the other hand, an entrepreneurial mindset that embraces flexibility allows for innovative problem-solving and the ability to seize new possibilities. By learning from the mistakes of

others, you can gain insights into areas where flexibility is crucial, such as adjusting your business model, exploring different markets, or adapting to technological advancements.

Learning from Business Mistakes:
Mistakes are an inevitable part of the entrepreneurial journey. However, what sets successful entrepreneurs apart is their ability to learn from these mistakes and use them as stepping stones to growth. By studying the failures of others, you gain valuable lessons without having to endure the same costly setbacks. Understanding how others have adapted and been flexible in the face of adversity can provide you with invaluable insights. It allows you to avoid common pitfalls, make informed decisions, and develop a resilient mindset that embraces change.

Conclusion:
In the ever-evolving world of entrepreneurship, adaptability and flexibility are essential qualities for success. As students, learning from the mistakes of others equips you with the knowledge and wisdom needed to navigate the challenges that lie ahead. By being adaptable, flexible, and open to change, you can position yourself as an agile entrepreneur ready to seize opportunities and overcome obstacles. Remember, adaptability and flexibility are not just traits, but skills that can be developed through continuous learning and a willingness to embrace failure as a stepping stone towards growth.

Building a Strong Support Network

One crucial aspect of entrepreneurship that is often overlooked is the importance of building a strong support network. As aspiring entrepreneurs, it is essential for students to recognize that they cannot succeed on their own. Learning from the mistakes of others, we understand that a robust support network can provide invaluable guidance, advice, and encouragement throughout the entrepreneurial journey.

Starting a business can be daunting, and setbacks are inevitable. However, having a solid support network can help students navigate through challenges and learn from others' experiences. This network can consist of mentors, fellow entrepreneurs, friends, family members, and even online communities dedicated to entrepreneurship. These individuals can provide insights, offer different perspectives, share their own mistakes, and provide emotional support during difficult times.

One of the most significant advantages of having a support network is the opportunity to learn from the mistakes of others. By connecting with experienced entrepreneurs who have already faced the hurdles that lie ahead, students can gain valuable insights into what works and what doesn't. Learning from others' mistakes allows students to avoid making the same errors and accelerates their learning curve.

Moreover, a strong support network can offer guidance and advice when students encounter unfamiliar situations. They can provide valuable feedback on business plans, marketing strategies, and even personal development. This network acts as a sounding board for ideas, helping students refine their concepts and make informed decisions.

In addition to practical advice, a support network can also provide emotional support, which is crucial when facing the inevitable challenges and setbacks that entrepreneurship brings. Surrounding oneself with like-minded individuals who understand the pressures and uncertainties of starting a business can boost morale and motivation. They can provide words of encouragement during tough times and celebrate successes, no matter how small.

To build a strong support network, students can start by reaching out to their existing connections, such as professors, alumni, and family members. Attending entrepreneurship events, workshops, and seminars can also provide opportunities to meet like-minded individuals. Joining online communities and forums dedicated to entrepreneurship can further expand the network, allowing students to connect with entrepreneurs from diverse backgrounds.

In conclusion, building a strong support network is a vital part of the entrepreneurial journey. By learning from the mistakes of others and seeking guidance, advice, and emotional support from a network of individuals, students can enhance their chances of success. Remember, entrepreneurship is not a solitary endeavor, and a strong support network can make all the difference in achieving your entrepreneurial goals.

Chapter 6: Strategies for Success

Developing a Growth Mindset

In the journey of entrepreneurship, mistakes are inevitable. As students venturing into the world of business, it is crucial to adopt a growth mindset that embraces failure as a stepping stone toward success. This subchapter aims to guide you through the process of developing a growth mindset and understanding the importance of learning from your mistakes.

A growth mindset is a fundamental attitude that recognizes challenges, setbacks, and even failures as opportunities for growth and improvement. Instead of viewing failure as a sign of incompetence, individuals with a growth mindset see it as a chance to learn, adapt, and ultimately succeed.

One of the key aspects of developing a growth mindset is embracing a positive mindset towards failure. Rather than being discouraged by missteps, students should view them as valuable learning experiences. By analyzing what went wrong and why, you can gain valuable insights that can guide your future endeavors.

Furthermore, developing resilience is crucial in nurturing a growth mindset. Entrepreneurship is filled with ups and downs, and it is essential to bounce back from failures and setbacks. Resilience allows you to persevere, learn from mistakes, and continue moving forward with renewed determination.

Another important aspect of developing a growth mindset is seeking feedback and learning from others. Surrounding yourself with mentors, peers, and industry experts who can provide guidance and constructive criticism can accelerate your learning curve. Embrace feedback as an opportunity for growth and improvement, and actively seek it out.

Moreover, it is essential to cultivate a passion for continuous learning. Successful entrepreneurs understand that knowledge and skills are ever-evolving, and they proactively seek opportunities to expand their understanding. Embrace a curious mindset, engage in ongoing learning, and stay updated with industry trends to remain adaptable and relevant.

Lastly, maintaining a growth mindset requires self-belief and a positive attitude. Believe in your abilities, trust the process, and have faith in your capacity to learn and grow. Cultivate a positive outlook that sees failures as temporary setbacks rather than permanent roadblocks.

In conclusion, developing a growth mindset is vital for students embarking on the path of entrepreneurship. Viewing mistakes as valuable opportunities for learning, embracing resilience, seeking feedback, nurturing a passion for continuous learning, and maintaining a positive attitude are all essential components of a growth mindset. By adopting these principles, you can learn from your mistakes and propel yourself towards success in the world of business.

Continuous Learning and Professional Development

In the fast-paced and ever-evolving world of entrepreneurship, one of the key factors that set successful entrepreneurs apart is their commitment to continuous learning and professional development. This subchapter explores the importance of embracing a growth mindset, learning from mistakes, and continuously improving oneself in the entrepreneurial journey.

The journey of entrepreneurship is often marked by ups and downs, challenges, and setbacks. However, it is through these mistakes and failures that valuable lessons are learned. As students, you have the opportunity to learn from the mistakes of experienced entrepreneurs who have walked the path before you. By understanding the failures and missteps of others, you can avoid making similar mistakes and accelerate your own learning curve.

Learning from mistakes is not about dwelling on the past or feeling discouraged by failures. Instead, it is about extracting the valuable lessons from each experience and using them to fuel personal and professional growth. In this subchapter, you will discover how to analyze mistakes, identify patterns, and develop strategies to prevent their recurrence. By adopting a proactive approach to learning from mistakes, you will be better equipped to navigate challenges and make informed decisions in your entrepreneurial endeavors.

Furthermore, continuous learning and professional development go hand in hand with personal growth. As an aspiring entrepreneur, you should constantly seek opportunities to expand your knowledge, skills, and network. This subchapter will delve into various avenues for professional development, including attending workshops, conferences, and networking events, as well as engaging in online courses, podcasts, and mentorship programs. By actively seeking out these opportunities, you will enhance your entrepreneurial skill set, gain valuable insights, and foster connections with like-minded individuals in your niche.

Remember, the entrepreneurial journey is a lifelong learning process. Embracing continuous learning and professional development not only equips you with the tools and knowledge needed to succeed, but it also cultivates a growth mindset that fuels your passion and drive. By learning from the mistakes of others and continually investing in your personal growth, you will position yourself for success in the dynamic world of entrepreneurship.

So, grab a pen, take notes, and get ready to embark on a journey of continuous learning and professional development. Your entrepreneurial success starts here.

Finding Mentors and Role Models

Subchapter: Finding Mentors and Role Models

Introduction:
In the journey of entrepreneurship, one cannot underestimate the power of mentors and role models. Learning from their experiences, mistakes, and successes can significantly impact your own entrepreneurial path. In this subchapter, we will explore the importance of finding mentors and role models and how they can help you learn from business mistakes. Whether you are a student just starting out or someone looking to enhance their entrepreneurial skills, this chapter will provide valuable insights and advice.

The Power of Mentors:
Mentors play a crucial role in shaping your entrepreneurial mindset. They are experienced individuals who can guide you through the challenges and hurdles you may encounter. They provide practical advice, share their own mistakes, and offer valuable insights that can save you from potential pitfalls. By having a mentor, you can learn from their mistakes and avoid making them yourself. A mentor can also provide a fresh perspective, challenge your ideas, and push you to grow as an entrepreneur.

Finding the Right Role Models:
Role models are individuals who have achieved success in the entrepreneurial world. They serve as a source of inspiration and motivation, showing you what is possible with dedication and hard work. When choosing role models, it is important to look beyond their achievements and focus on their journey. Understanding the mistakes

they made and how they overcame them can provide invaluable lessons for your own entrepreneurial endeavors.

Learning from Mistakes:
Mistakes are an inevitable part of the entrepreneurial journey. However, learning from the mistakes of others can save you time, money, and frustration. Mentors and role models can share their own failures and the lessons they learned from them. By studying their experiences, you can identify potential pitfalls, develop strategies to mitigate risks, and make informed decisions. Embracing the mindset of learning from mistakes will not only help you avoid similar errors but also foster resilience and adaptability.

Developing Mentorship Relationships:
To find mentors and role models, start by networking within your industry or entrepreneurial community. Attend conferences, join relevant organizations, and seek out individuals who align with your goals and values. Approach them with humility, respect, and a genuine desire to learn. Building a strong mentorship relationship takes time and effort, so be prepared to invest in the relationship and show your commitment to personal growth.

Conclusion:
Finding mentors and role models is an essential part of the entrepreneurial journey. Learning from their experiences, mistakes, and successes can accelerate your own growth as an entrepreneur. By embracing their guidance and wisdom, you can navigate the challenges of entrepreneurship with greater confidence and make informed decisions. Remember, success is not just about avoiding mistakes but also learning from them.

Chapter 7: The Road to Entrepreneurial Success

Setting Realistic Goals and Milestones

In the journey of entrepreneurship, setting realistic goals and milestones is essential for success. As students venturing into the world of business, it is crucial to learn from the mistakes made by others and understand the importance of setting attainable targets. This subchapter aims to guide you through the process of setting realistic goals and milestones, enabling you to avoid the pitfalls that many entrepreneurs encounter.

When starting a business, it is easy to get carried away with big dreams and lofty ambitions. While having grand aspirations is commendable, setting unrealistic goals can quickly lead to frustration and disappointment. Instead, focus on creating goals that are challenging yet attainable. By setting achievable targets, you can maintain motivation and ensure continued progress.

To begin, identify your long-term vision for the business. What do you hope to achieve in the next five or ten years? Once you have a clear picture of your ultimate goal, break it down into smaller milestones. These milestones act as stepping stones towards your larger objective, providing a sense of direction and accomplishment along the way. Remember, Rome wasn't built in a day, and neither will your business.

When setting goals and milestones, it is crucial to be specific and measurable. Vague statements like "increase sales" or "expand customer base" lack clarity and make it difficult to track progress. Instead, set precise targets such as "increase sales by 10% in the next quarter" or "acquire 100 new customers by the end of the year." By defining your goals and attaching specific metrics, you can measure your progress accurately.

Furthermore, it is essential to set realistic timelines for achieving each milestone. Be mindful of the resources, manpower, and external factors that may influence the time required to reach your goals. Rushing through milestones can result in compromised quality, while extended timelines may lead to stagnation. Strive for a balance that allows for steady growth and adaptability.

Lastly, always reassess and adjust your goals and milestones as your business evolves. Market conditions, customer preferences, and industry trends are constantly changing, and your goals must align with these dynamics. Regularly evaluate your progress, celebrate achievements, and modify targets as necessary. Flexibility and resilience are key attributes of successful entrepreneurs.

As students learning from the mistakes of others, setting realistic goals and milestones is a vital skill to acquire. By setting attainable targets, breaking them down into measurable milestones, and regularly reassessing your progress, you can navigate the entrepreneurial journey with confidence. Remember, success is not achieved overnight, but through consistent effort and the ability to learn from your mistakes and adapt.

Perseverance and Resilience in the Face of Setbacks

In the ever-evolving world of entrepreneurship, setbacks and failures are inevitable. As aspiring entrepreneurs, it is crucial to understand that success is not a linear path but rather a journey filled with twists and turns. It is through these setbacks that we learn some of the most valuable lessons in entrepreneurship.

Perseverance and resilience are two essential traits that every entrepreneur must possess to overcome setbacks and turn them into stepping stones towards success. These qualities enable us to navigate through challenges with determination and bounce back from failures stronger than ever.

One of the greatest mistakes we can make as students of entrepreneurship is to view setbacks as roadblocks or signs of incompetence. Rather, setbacks should be seen as opportunities for growth and self-improvement. Each setback is a chance to reevaluate our strategies, learn from our mistakes, and emerge stronger.

When faced with a setback, the first step is to take a moment to reflect and understand what went wrong. It is essential to analyze the situation objectively, identifying the root cause of the setback. This process of self-reflection allows us to gain valuable insights and prevents us from repeating the same mistakes in the future.

After understanding the cause of the setback, it is crucial to maintain a positive mindset and stay motivated. Entrepreneurship is a rollercoaster ride, and setbacks are just a part of the journey. By cultivating a resilient attitude, we can bounce back from failures, learn from them, and move forward towards our goals.

Perseverance is the driving force that keeps us going despite setbacks. It is the ability to stay committed to our vision and goals, even when faced with obstacles. Perseverance pushes us to keep trying new strategies, exploring alternative solutions, and taking calculated risks.

Learning from the mistakes of others is another valuable lesson in entrepreneurship. By studying the experiences of successful entrepreneurs who have faced setbacks, we can gain insights into their resilience and perseverance. Their stories can inspire us to push through our own setbacks and keep moving forward.

In conclusion, setbacks are an inevitable part of the entrepreneurial journey. However, by embracing perseverance and resilience, we can transform setbacks into opportunities for growth and learning. Remember, every setback is a stepping stone towards success. So, stay motivated, analyze your mistakes, and keep pushing forward on your entrepreneurial path.

Celebrating Achievements and Learning from Successes

In our journey as entrepreneurs, it is crucial to not only acknowledge and celebrate our achievements but also learn valuable lessons from our successes. As students of entrepreneurship, we must understand that failure is not the only teacher; success can also be a great mentor if we are willing to learn from it.

Celebrating achievements is important as it boosts morale and motivation. When we accomplish a goal or reach a milestone, it is essential to take a moment to acknowledge our hard work and dedication. Celebrating achievements not only fosters a sense of accomplishment but also encourages us to set new goals and push ourselves further.

However, it is equally important to delve deeper into our successes and extract valuable lessons. Success can sometimes blind us, making us overlook the factors that contributed to it. By analyzing our achievements, we can identify the strategies, decisions, and actions that led to positive outcomes. These insights can then be applied to future endeavors, increasing the likelihood of success.

Learning from successes helps us build a solid foundation for our entrepreneurial journey. It allows us to understand what works well and what doesn't, enabling us to refine our approach and make informed decisions. By studying successful ventures, we can gain valuable insights into effective marketing techniques, customer engagement strategies, and innovative solutions that have proven to be successful. This knowledge empowers us to replicate those strategies and adapt them to our own business ventures.

Moreover, learning from successes also helps us avoid complacency. Success can sometimes lead to a false sense of security, making us overlook potential risks or become resistant to change. By actively seeking lessons from our successes, we can remain vigilant and open to new opportunities for growth and improvement.

As students in the field of entrepreneurship, it is important to embrace both failure and success as valuable learning experiences. While failures teach us resilience and the importance of perseverance, successes offer us insights into effective strategies and approaches. By celebrating achievements and learning from successes, we can continuously evolve as entrepreneurs, armed with the knowledge and skills needed to navigate the dynamic business landscape successfully. So, let us not only learn from our mistakes but also celebrate our achievements and leverage them as stepping stones towards future success.

Chapter 8: Conclusion

Final Thoughts on Learning from Business Mistakes

In our journey through the world of entrepreneurship, we have explored numerous business mistakes and the valuable lessons they offer. As students pursuing knowledge and growth, it is crucial to understand the importance of learning from these mistakes and applying those lessons to our own ventures. In this final subchapter, we will delve deeper into the significance of embracing failures and extracting wisdom from them.

Mistakes are an inevitable part of any entrepreneurial journey. They can be disheartening and demotivating, but they also present us with an opportunity to learn and improve. As students, we must recognize that failure is not the end but rather a stepping stone towards success. It is through these mistakes that we gain experience, develop resilience, and refine our strategies.

One of the key takeaways from this book is the notion that mistakes are not to be feared, but rather embraced. Each failure is a chance to analyze and identify what went wrong and why. By dissecting these mistakes, we can uncover valuable insights that will help us navigate similar challenges in the future. Remember, the most successful entrepreneurs are the ones who have experienced failure and learned from it.

Furthermore, learning from mistakes is not limited to our own experiences; we can also learn from the mistakes of others. This book has provided us with a plethora of case studies and real-life examples, showcasing the errors made by renowned entrepreneurs. By studying these stories, we can gain a deeper understanding of the potential pitfalls in business and avoid making similar mistakes ourselves.

As students, it is imperative that we adopt a growth mindset. Instead of dwelling on our failures, we should view them as opportunities for growth and improvement. Every mistake is a chance to refine our skills, reassess our strategies, and develop a better understanding of the entrepreneurial landscape.

In conclusion, the path to success in entrepreneurship is paved with failures and mistakes. Embracing these missteps and learning from them is essential for personal and professional growth. By studying the mistakes of others, reflecting on our own failures, and adopting a growth mindset, we can transform setbacks into stepping stones towards success. As students, we have the unique advantage of being able to learn from the mistakes of others and apply those lessons in our own entrepreneurial endeavors. So, let us embark on our journey armed with the knowledge gained from this book, ready to make our mark on the world of business.

www.ingramcontent.com/pod-product-compliance
Lightning Source LLC
LaVergne TN
LVHW051921060526
838201LV00060B/4120